The Tyring House

Lynn Thornton

Helen,
 Best wishes,
 Lynn

MULFRAN PRESS

First published 2020 by Poet's House Pamphlets,
Oxford, 14 Kineton Road, Oxford OX1 4PG
jennylewis.org.uk

Poet's House Pamphlets, Oxford
is an imprint of Mulfran Press,
2, Aber Street, Cardiff CF11 7AG, UK
www.mulfran.co.uk

Cover design by Frances Kiernan
www.franceskiernan.co.uk
Layout by Oliver Harrison
harrison.oliver@gmail.com

Dalton Printers, Cardiff.
www.daltonprinters.co.uk

ISBN 978-1-907327-36-0

for Felicity
my granddaughter

Acknowledgements

'Viola' was published in the *Bedford Square Anthology*, number 5.
'Penelope' was published in *Sentinel Literary Quarterly*.

I would like to thank Jenny Lewis for her generous support and
inspiration and Frances Kiernan for designing this pamphlet;
Francis Warner who first started me on this journey, and for the
encouragement of many fellow poets, including Catherine Faulds,
Margot Myers, Lucy Ingrams, Jennie Carr, Sarah Watkinson,
Elizabeth Thompson, Charles Atkinson; and Brian, my husband,
for his patience and encouragement.

Contents

The Tyring House

smells of musk
sweat
tallow thick
air

where we lurch
for a sword
a crown
a clown's cap

our bodies
pressed close
waiting for
the call

one line
prompts
through
a rough curtain

then out into
sunlight
in full gaze
we plunder
a scene
with sawing

an off-key
Cleopatra
a fat Hamlet
sweating in
a graveyard

running the risk
of burlesque
a merry wife
turning a trick

a hunchback
trailing a leg
a fat knight's
stuffed belly
saggy

faces turned up
yelling
like
bear baiters
waiting for
a slip
on the tightrope
a pratfall

every performance
harder
to balance
on a good day
we get away
with

an exit jig

Cordelia

i

I take
my silence
to me

swallow
it whole

it shall be
my disobedience

it shall be
my dowry

it shall be
my all

the noise of it will raise an army.

Cordelia

ii

Leaves fall early this autumn
apples are picked and stored

birds swoop over cornfields
peck grain left by scythes.

I imagine them feasting on your
lands, flocks of starlings, crows,

gulls, careless of boundaries,
whilst I remain here, corseted

in a foreign tongue, making the best
of it, watching the seasons, always

conscious of the sea that separates us.
From my window I hear the ebb tide

as it slips away; dusk fringes the land
the last light silvers an owl's wing

as it plunges, swift as a knife towards
a whisper in the stubble.

Lear

is lofted
higher and higher, his pale fingers fasten
on nothing

below him,
two crocodile daughters arrange their faces
in shadow, smile

one sways
but doesn't fall, somewhere she feels a hinge
begin to give

the other
ram rod straight, strains to hear a kite's call,
frets her sleeve

the third
white-knuckled hands tight around her ribcage,
to let go would be

to let all out
spool away, like a winding sheet, leaving her
naked

above them
their father's feet, tiny in kid leather, assault
the air

nothing
to rest on, whilst the one with the bright coxcomb
goes slipshod.

Lear's Fool

An unpainted landscape
is all he has to offer as he pirouettes close to the king
plugs the walls with sacking against an east wind

that whistles through skeletal trees,
beyond them the sea moans in its moorings, as the tide
turns it sings a troubadour's tune

a tune he would follow
but the old man whines in his sleep, flails his arms
to the empty air and yells out his name.

He shrinks into shadows
of tumbling pictures, great log fires, steaming dogs, dark
tapestries of war draped on palace walls,

props for his dreams, for this rattler of tales,
this riddler, who had once left the stars amazed when he'd
pushed a great wheel uphill, the king cracking his whip after him
and screaming

Ophelia

I am distorted in moving water, stranded
on a stone or liberated

           like a kite

swooping low, or a high-wire artiste stretching
every muscle tensed, for another's hand

           almost touching

but not quite; always the reflection of upturned faces
flaring round a circus ring

           waiting for me

to miss my mark, my fingers to slip in the folding
stream, a quiver on the surface

           punctured by stars

Fortinbras

Our paths crossed once
at Wittenberg, in a bierkeller;
you were merry, combative even,
climbing onto a table to make a point
until the barman pulled you back -

but you didn't care a jot for authority,
you marched out into the night, stood
in a freezing square, shouting at the stars,
you were all purpose and defiance, kicking
at anything that moved, even shadows.

Here at Elsinore,

where the unsayable
blooms like promiscuous orchids
where anything said can be unsaid
where blood spreads over rough floors
where the air is sticky like molasses
where the early light seems tawdry
except when it catches your hand
slender and white as a girl's, resting
on your chest, as though signalling
a mid-sentence pause -

you look almost beatific among the dead
and speechless living; your eyes wide as though
surprised to see me here, a walk-on part
in your great tragedy.

Will

calm the day
and lustrous clear
the river ran through
banks of heartsease

strange the day
he first walked

in the herb garden
its fragrant air
lulled him
to indolence

to unravelling memory
to words on the slide
to drinking spiced wine
to waking long after
cock crow

for the first time

Viola

A trunk in an attic, a foil
against moths, now spills

its gaudy contents to the light
that captures the rupture of shot silk
before the dust settles on tight velvet
breeches for a loose-limbed Viola with
husband, children, and she, the perfect wife.

Where are you now
in a ritzy café on the Bahnhofstrasse
or peering out across the lake
for the last ferry of the night?

Malvolio

They say the estate has run to rack and ruin
since my incarceration, but I hold my tongue

talk only to shadows, words bleat to empty
air, mice mock me from behind the wainscot.

The court giggled as I passed in my new motley,
at the aching smile I wore for her sake.

But I have ink and paper, a fine cheval mirror
for company. What a fix. Malvolio silenced

sitting alone at the writing desk, she bought him,
his legs folded beneath, like yellow fiddle sticks

Feste

will always come in answer
to your text, never keeps the customer waiting
from Rickmansworth to Brent Cross.

He'll leap into his polished Mini Cooper
red with a white racing stripe, he prides himself
on the speed he wings it from one gig to the next.

And the moment his foot's in the door he won't miss
a beat with his sparkling repartee, he'll tell a dubious
tale or two and never mention money 'till he leaves.

And you'd never guess he'd just left a dingy basement
flat, so dark you can hardly see the mould blooming half
way up the wall or the coat of faded motley on a plastic
hanger by the door.

Paulina

She folds linen neatly into piles
with the calmness of a nun

this is what she's good at
this is what she's perfected

this her preferred occupation
this is what stops her listening

to angry voices drifting up from the yard
to a fool's cry like a trinket jangling

on the wind, to a blackbird's plaintive
song to her mistress's weeping

to the chip, chip, chip of a sculptor's chisel
fretting away at stone,

to her own heart's pounding

Sicilia

I think of their summer palace

cool colonnades where peacocks
                    trail their feathers
even in winter; the sweet smell of
                    rosemary and sage,
think I hear the promises they make,
                    their son as he rides
his rocking horse over mountains of snow.

These are the good days, the days
                    when they stroll from
room to room, hand in hand, hear bird song
                    float up from the courtyard
the call of shepherds from the valley.

All this before she walks alone into
                    their bedroom, feels
the heat of a hand's imprint on hers
                    burning like a brand
or notices the bruises on her arm bunched
                    like grapes where he'd
flung her from him; or hear her son's cry
                    as he falls.

A Villa in Milan

A map of tiles
    in my father's house shows all the contours

of our island home
    bounded by rough seas and dolphin-crested waves

a border of a thousand
    hectic flowers, his residue of empire

out of place here among
    satin drapes and gilded shutters

paintings of exotic places we never visit
    but talk of in whispers when someone dies.

I map them in my mind, speak their names aloud,
    Alentejo, Porto, Andalusia, dream

of ochre-baked streets, in winter, hail-pitted
    with rain. Here, outside my window dry-headed

sunflowers buckle in the breeze, on his island wild orchids
    are scattered like weeds.

Ariel's Complaint

My limbs are whisper thin
my hair like spun flax; I can slide through
keyholes, hang unnoticed from an orchid's tongue

        but I long

for an arm strong enough
to stretch a bow, send an arrow to its mark
he won't agree, thinks I'll pack my bags

        and run

his mantra; magic's the only strength – not smoke
and mirrors, sleight of hand – his art delivered,
swift as lightening, by me

        his imagined thing

gifting me
the power to create storms, tear up trees,
topple towers, part waves, wreck ships,
ripen wild strawberries

        in the snow –

but all I want is the rude strength of a Caliban,
muscle to confront a mob, come out the victor in
a late-night brawl, feel my feet firmly

        on the ground.

Caliban

You want to take my photograph?

I'll move out of the shadows then you'll see
my strong chin, my deep-set eyes and, some say,
generous mouth.

But don't show my hands, they're too capable
and ready to take a swing at anyone who comes
too close or, uninvited, looks into my cell.

See, I've decked it out with mermaid's tails,
swathes of gossamer caught at the ebbtide; my bed
is draped in robes of iridescence.

Peacocks wake me at first light and when the moon
is full I become someone else.

Antigone

A cacophony of days and nights play out
beneath her window, the one that looks onto
the hills where the crows wheel round and round
their cawing almost mellifluous in the warm air

drowning out the flute player in the square
no one seems to notice them except her, hypnotically
plaiting and un-plaiting the fine threads of tasselled
cord that tomorrow she will secure to an iron lintel,

climb down, drop soundlessly to the street below
and run for all she's worth along an unmarked track,
up the hillside until she finds what's left of the crows'
feast rotting in the sun then, and only then, will she

call out his name, again, and again as she piles stones
into a makeshift monument.

Penelope

She'd have known him anywhere
by his height, by his chest barrelled
like an ox, by his scars, by the way
he looked at her, by the way he stumbled
as he mounted the stairs.

Like a statue she stood by the fire,
hoped it would unfreeze her veins,
warm her to welcome him, but when she
opened her mouth nothing came out, certainly
no sound he could recognize.

I am come, he said, not looking at her
but at the mirror that hung above her head,
in it he saw his face crumble as if the silvering
had slipped, but not before it had imperfectly
caught the birds she'd woven, taking flight.

She remembers the doves

                       in a land where sharp-eyed women
sew calico shrouds by smoking fires

she remembers the doves in a land where flowers bloom
on tapestries and forests are marble

she remembers the doves as she watches the sea churn,
digs her fingers into rock fissures when the wind pulls

she remembers the doves on days when the shuttle jams
and the yarn frays, pools round her feet in chains

she remembers the doves when the air is clogged with cries
of homecoming, women weeping

she remembers the doves the day they took flight, still hears
their soft cooing, their breasts golden in sunlight